Healthy Habits

by Rebecca Weber

Content Adviser: September Kirby, CNS, MS, RN,
Instructor, Health Promotion and Wellness,
South Dakota State University

Reading Adviser: Rosemary G. Palmer, Ph.D.,
Department of Literacy, College of Education,
Boise State University

Spyglass
BOOKS

COMPASS POINT BOOKS

Minneapolis, Minnesota

Compass Point Books
3109 West 50th Street, #115
Minneapolis, MN 55410

Visit Compass Point Books on the Internet at *www.compasspointbooks.com*
or e-mail your request to *custserv@compasspointbooks.com*

Photographs ©: Digital Vision, cover, 13; Comstock, 4, 5, 20 (top); Jose Luis Pelaez, Inc./
Corbis, 6, 7, 20 (bottom); Michael Keller/Corbis, 8; Index Stock Imagery/SW Productions, 9;
Brand X Pictures, 10; Corbis, 11; George Disario/Corbis, 12; EyeWire, 14; PhotoDisc, 15, 18,
19, 21; LWA-Dann Tardif/Corbis, 16; BananaStock, 17.

Editor: Patricia Stockland
Photo Researcher: Marcie C. Spence
Designer: Jaime Martens

Library of Congress Cataloging-in-Publication Data
Weber, Rebecca.
  Healthy habits / by Rebecca Weber.
      p. cm. — (Spyglass books)
  Includes bibliographical references and index.
  Contents: A healthy day—Good foods—Clean and shiny—Teeth talk—Playing hard—
Don't dry out—Snack attack—Deep sleep.
  ISBN 0-7565-0627-1 (hardcover)
  1. Health—Juvenile literature. 2. Health behavior—Juvenile literature. [1. Health.]
  I. Title. II. Series.
  RA777.W43 2004
  613—dc22   2003014467

Contents

NOTE: Glossary words are in **bold** the first time they appear.

A Healthy Day

There are many things you can do to keep your body healthy.

Think about your day. How can you be healthy?

Out of Gas

If a car runs out of gas, it cannot work. If your body does not get enough rest or good food, it cannot work either.

Good Food

Eating breakfast keeps you healthy.

Your body needs food to work well. Breakfast gives you *energy* after sleeping all night.

Eat Many Foods

Juice and fruit will give you energy right away. Cereal and toast will give you energy for several hours.

Clean and Shiny

Taking care of your skin keeps you healthy.

Wash with warm water. Use soap, but don't scrub too hard. This gets rid of all the *germs* and dirt.

Safe in the Sun

Wear sunscreen when you go outside. This will help protect your skin from the sun.

9

Teeth Talk

Brushing your teeth keeps you healthy.

Brush your teeth at least two times a day. Use dental *floss* to get rid of food between your teeth.

Sugary Snacks

Sugar can harm your teeth. Always try to brush after eating something sweet.

Playing Hard

Exercise keeps you healthy.

Play games with your friends. Run, jump, or dance. Get moving for at least 30 minutes. Have fun!

Strong Muscles

Exercise makes your muscles strong. Your heart is a muscle. Each time you exercise, your heart has a chance to get stronger, too.

Don't Dry Out

Drinking water keeps you healthy.

Your body needs water more than food or anything else. Drink water all day.

Getting Thirsty

Drink before you feel thirsty. Thirst is your body's way of telling you that it has been without water for too long.

Snack Attack

Having a snack keeps you healthy. When you get hungry, eat **nutritious** foods. Junk foods make you tired. Eat a sandwich or some fruit for long-lasting energy.

Don't Eat and Run

Try not to eat one hour before exercising. Food may make you *cramp* or feel sick when you start moving.

Deep Sleep

Getting enough sleep keeps you healthy.

Even after a healthy day, your body needs rest. Sleep is when a body *repairs* itself. It ends a full day of healthy habits!

Time to Sleep

Every living animal needs to sleep. Even fish sleep. They float in the water.

Fun Facts

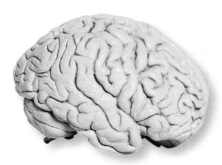

- Your brain has to tell your body how to relax and fall asleep.

- People have not always had toothpaste. They used to brush their teeth with ground up chalk, ashes, or even baking soda.

- Sports bars do not give your body any more energy than healthy food.

- Strong muscles don't just help you play longer. They can help keep your body from getting hurt while you play.

- Fresh fruits and vegetables have more *vitamins* than frozen. Frozen fruits and vegetables have more vitamins than canned.

21

Glossary

cramp–when muscles tighten up and feel painful

energy–the power that lets something or someone do work

floss–a long, thin string

germs–very small things that can make you sick

nutritious–helps living things grow by giving food or vitamins

repairs–to make something work again, or to put back together something that is broken

vitamins–something in food that is needed for good health

Learn More

Books

Hausherr, Rosmarie. *What Food Is This?* New York: Scholastic, 1994.

Thomas, Pat. *My Amazing Body: A First Look at Health and Fitness.* New York: Barron's, 2002.

On the Web

For more information on Healthy Habits, use FactHound to track down Web sites related to this book.

1. Go to *www.compasspointbooks.com/ facthound*
2. Type in this book ID: 0756506271
3. Click on the *Fetch It* button. Your trusty FactHound will fetch the best Web sites for you!

Index

GR: I
Word Count: 193

From Rebecca Weber

The world is such a great place! I love teaching kids how to take care of themselves and take care of nature.